P9-DMP-650

WHERE IS MY STATE?

by Robin Nelson

first step nonfiction

Lerner Publications Company · Minneapolis

I live in a **state.**

A state is a piece of land
in a country.

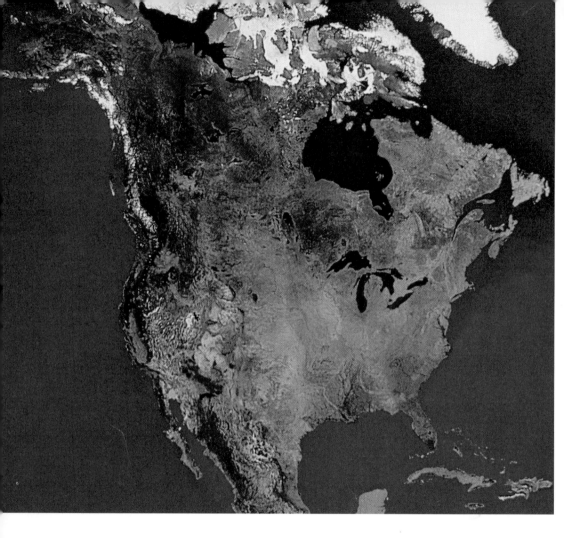

The country I live in is the
United States of America.

My country has 50 states.

A state has many towns
where families live.

A state has cities, **suburbs**,
and the country.

There is a **border** around
each state.

I can find my state
on a **map**.

A family can live in a state
in the mountains.

A family can live in a state
on the **plains**.

A family can live in a state
in the desert.

A family can live
in a state by water.

A family can live in a state
by the Arctic.

A family can live in a state
in the middle of the ocean.

Where is my state?

My state is in my country,
where I live with my family.

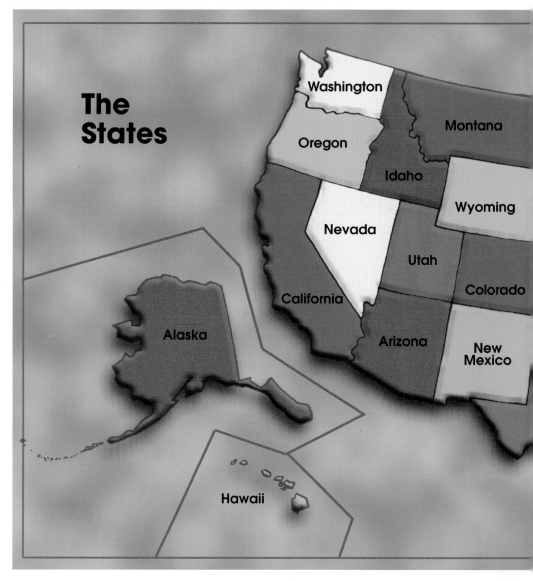

The States

Washington

Montana

Oregon

Idaho

Wyoming

Nevada

Utah

Colorado

California

Alaska

Arizona

New Mexico

Hawaii

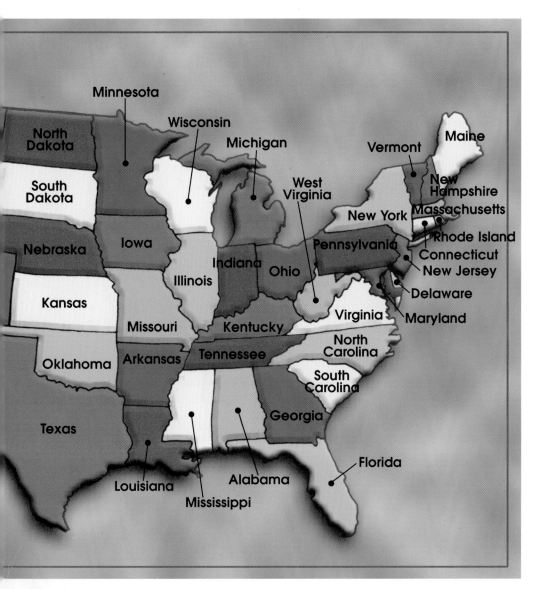

Minnesota

North Dakota

Wisconsin

Michigan

Vermont

Maine

South Dakota

West Virginia

New Hampshire

New York

Massachusetts

Nebraska

Iowa

Pennsylvania

Rhode Island

Connecticut

Indiana

Ohio

New Jersey

Illinois

Kansas

Delaware

Missouri

Kentucky

Virginia

Maryland

Oklahoma

Arkansas

Tennessee

North Carolina

South Carolina

Texas

Georgia

Louisiana

Alabama

Florida

Mississippi

19

State Facts

 The first state to become part of the United States of America was Delaware. It became a state in 1787.

 The last state to become part of the United States of America was Hawaii. It became a state in 1959.

 The biggest state is Alaska.

 The smallest state is Rhode Island.

The state with the largest number of people is California.

 The state with the smallest number of people is Wyoming.

 In the United States, the 50 states are divided into 7 regions. These regions are New England, the Middle Atlantic, the Southeast, the Southwest, the Midwest, the Rocky Mountains, and the Pacific Coast.

Glossary

 border – an imaginary line between one area of land and another

 map – a drawing of an area showing borders, towns, water, and mountains

 plains – large, flat areas of land

 state – one of many areas of land that make up a country

 suburbs – areas on or close to the outer edge of a city

Index

The photographs in this book are reproduced through the courtesy of: © Todd Strand/Independent Picture Service, pp. 2, 9, 22 (second from top); © David Vinyard/Photo Network, p. 3; © Earth Imaging/Stone, p. 4; © Corbis Royalty Free, p. 6; © Jeff Greenberg/Visuals Unlimited, pp. 7, 22 (bottom); © Steve Strickland/Visuals Unlimited, p. 10; © Phil Schermeister/Corbis, pp. 11, 22 (middle); © Wolfgang Kaehler, p. 12; © Mark E. Gibson/Visuals Unlimited, p. 13; © Hank Andrews/Visuals Unlimited, p. 14; © Paul J. Buklarewicz, p. 15; © Jeff Greenberg/Photo Agora, p. 16; © Gerard Fritz/Photo Agora, p. 17.

Lerner Publications Company
A division of Lerner Publishing Group
241 First Avenue North
Minneapolis, MN 55401 U.S.A.

Website address: www.lernerbooks.com

Library of Congress Cataloging-in-Publication Data

Nelson, Robin, 1971–
    Where is my state? / by Robin Nelson.
        p.   cm. — (First step nonfiction)
    Includes index.
    ISBN: 0–8225–0191–0 (lib. bdg. : alk. paper)
    1. U.S. states—Juvenile literature. 2. United States—Geography—Juvenile literature.
    3. Regionalism—United States—Juvenile literature [1. United States—Geography.]
    I. Title. II. Series.
    E180.N45 2002
    917.3—dc21   2001000964

Manufactured in the United States of America
1 2 3 4 5 6 – AM – 07 06 05 04 03 02